ANIMAL SENSES

HOW ANIMALS SEE, HEAR, TASTE, SMELL AND FEEL

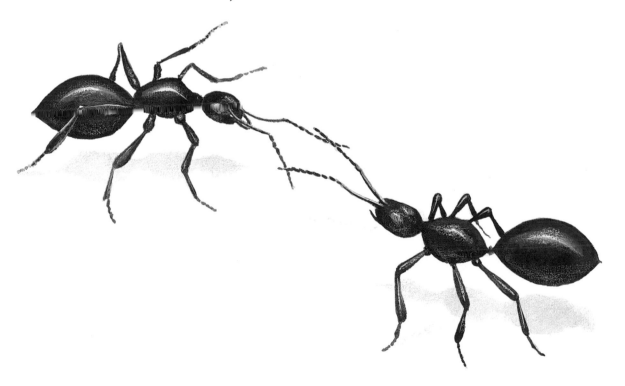

WRITTEN BY PAMELA HICKMAN

ILLUSTRATED BY PAT STEPHENS

Kids Can Press

I'd like to thank Valerie Hussey and Ricky Englander at Kids Can Press for their input and vision as this project changed course over many months. Thanks also to my editors Laurie Wark and Trudee Romanek and to Marie Bartholomew for the great design. The outstanding wildlife illustrations by Pat Stephens bring the book to life and I thank Pat for her hard work and amazing detail.

For Hazel and Jacqueline Hunter

Text © 1998 by Pamela Hickman
Illustrations © 1998 by Pat Stephens

Edited by Laurie Wark and Trudee Romanek
Designed by Marie Bartholomew

Printed and bound in China

CM   98 09 8 7 6 5 4 3 2
CM PA   98 09 8 7 6 5 4 3 2

Kids Can Press acknowledges the financial support of the Ontario Arts Council, the Canada Council for the Arts and the Government of Canada, through the BPIDP, for our publishing activity.

Canadian Cataloguing in Publication Data

Hickman, Pamela

Animal senses : how animals see, hear, taste, smell and feel

Includes index.
ISBN-13: 978-1-55074-423-1 (bound)
ISBN-10: 1-55074-423-2 (bound)

ISBN-13: 978-1-55074-425-5 (pbk.)
ISBN-10: 1-55074-425-9 (pbk.)

1. Senses and sensation – Juvenile literature.
I. Stephens, Pat. II. Title.

QP434.H52 1998   j573.8'7   C97-931623-5

Published in Canada by:
Kids Can Press Ltd.
29 Birch Avenue
Toronto, ON M4V 1E2

Published in the U.S. by:
Kids Can Press Ltd.
2250 Military Rd.
Tonawanda, NY 14150

www.kidscanpress.com

Kids Can Press is a **Corus** Entertainment company

Contents

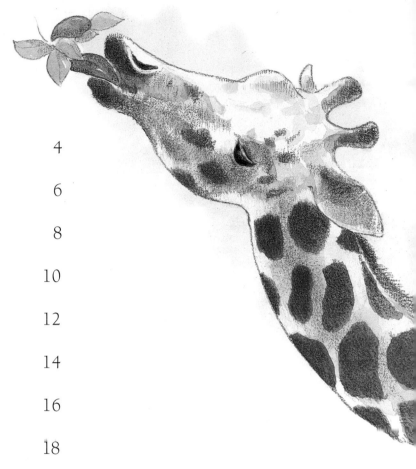

Introduction

Imagine if your eyes were on two long stalks and you could turn them all around to see, and flip them inside out to shut them. That's what a snail's eyes are like. Or what if you stuck your tongue out to smell the air, as a snake does? You might taste your dinner by walking on it, like a fly, or just feel it with your face to decide if it would be good enough to eat, the way a walrus does. And what if your ears were on your legs, like a cricket?

These things may sound strange to you, but they are all part of the amazing world of animal senses. In this book you will learn about the five senses — sight, hearing, smell, taste and touch — and other ways that animals sense their environment. Find out how their special senses help them survive, and compare their senses to yours. Did you know that a cow has four times as many taste buds as you? Or that a hawk can see ten times better than you can? There are lots of activities and experiments to help you discover why animals have these supersenses and what it would be like to taste things the way a butterfly does, see like a skunk, hear like a rabbit, and much more!

corn snake

Looking around

Look beside you without turning your head. You can see from side to side by moving your eyeballs, but birds can't move their eyes. A bird has to turn its whole head to look around. Birds have twice as many bones in their necks as you do, so their necks are flexible for all that turning. An owl can turn its head almost all the way around. It can even turn its head upside down. Some animals, such as this frog, can see what is behind them without turning their head. Read on to find out how they do this and why.

green frog

If you were a frog ...

- you would have very big eyes sticking up from your head.

- you could lie in the water with only your eyes sticking up above the surface. You could hunt and hide at the same time.

- your eyes would be turned to the sides and you could see almost all the way around your body without moving your head. This would help you look out for danger and food.

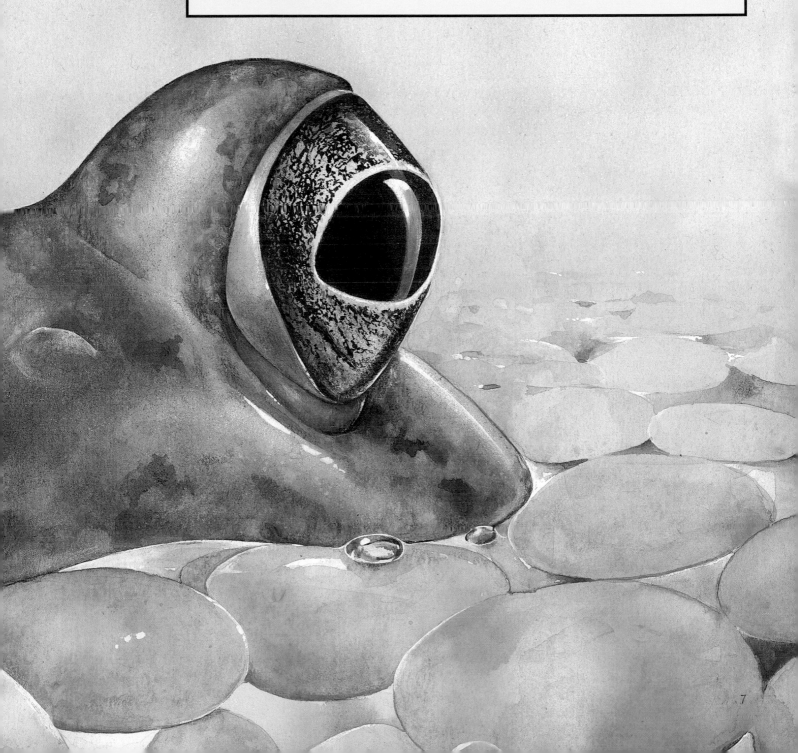

Giant-sized eyes

Your eyes stop growing when you are about seven years old even though the rest of your body keeps growing for many more years. Our eyes are just the right size for us — about 2.5 cm (1 in.) across — but some animals have huge eyes. Giant Squid have the largest eyes of any creature. Each eye is about as wide as this page. Large eyes let in more light than small ones, so they help a squid see better underwater, where it keeps watch for predators and prey.

Find your field of vision

The distance that you can see around your body without moving your head is called your field of vision. Find your field of vision by following these simple steps.

1. Stare ahead with your arms stretched out in front of you.

2. Continue to stare ahead. Slowly move your arms apart to the sides, keeping them straight.

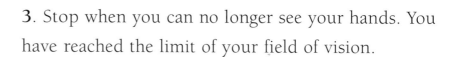

3. Stop when you can no longer see your hands. You have reached the limit of your field of vision.

You should discover that your field of vision ends where your arms are straight out on both sides of your body. Look at the picture of the frog's field of vision. If you stood in the same place as the frog, you would see only the part between the two lines. Deer, squirrels, dragonflies, rabbits and many fish also have large fields of vision. This helps them see predators that might be sneaking up on them from behind.

Try some eyes

Some animals can see better than people, while others hardly can see at all.
Try on some different eyes and see what you're missing.

1. Stand at one side of a room and look at something on the other side. Now look at the same object through a pair of binoculars to see how a hawk might see it. Hawks can see eight to ten times better than we can. This helps hawks that are flying or perched up high to see mice and other small animals on the ground.

2. Hold a kitchen colander up to your face and look through it. Through each hole you'll see a tiny part of what's in front of you. This is similar to how a lobster or an insect sees. You have only one lens in each of your eyes, but these creatures have many. Eyes like these are called compound eyes. Each eye is divided up into tiny sections that see little bits of the overall picture. Insects cannot focus their eyes, so they do not see images clearly. Our eyesight is about eighty times better than most insects'. Compound eyes are mainly good for seeing movement. Motion alerts the insect to danger or food.

Sightseeing

Most animals that hunt other animals have their eyes on the front of their head, like you. Both eyes focus on the same thing at the same time. This is called binocular vision. Binocular vision gives these predators better aim. Some animals have an eye on each side of their head. This is called monocular vision. Monocular vision helps an animal look for food with one eye and at the same time watch for danger with the other eye.

Eyewitness

Look at the eyes of these animals and guess which ones are predators.

lynx

woodcock

groundhog

wolf

porcupine

bear

Answers on page 40.

10

Test your binocular vision

Chameleons use their swiveling eyes to look for food and danger at the same time. When they find something to eat, they focus both eyes on it so they won't miss when they try to catch it. Try this experiment to see how important binocular vision is to a chameleon.

You'll need:

a party blower

a tall container, such as a 1-L (4-c.) yogurt container

a small piece of paper

1. Place the container upside down on a table.

2. Scrunch the paper into a little ball and put it on top of the container.

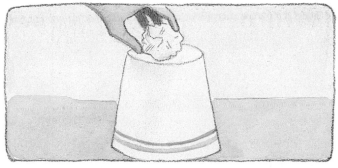

3. Crouch down so that you are level with the ball and within 15 cm (6 in.) of it. Put the party blower in your mouth. It works like the chameleon's long tongue, which is used to catch insects.

4. Close both eyes and count to ten. Open one eye, blow into the party blower and try to knock the paper off the container.

5. Repeat step 4, but this time open both eyes.

You should find that your aim is better with both eyes open — that is, when you use your binocular vision.

Night sight

If you go outside in the dark without a flashlight you probably bump into things, but many animals roam around at night without any problem. That's because they can see in the dark much better than you can. Many animals, including people, have two kinds of cells in their eyes: rods and cones. Rods help you see in the dark and cones help you see color. Animals that are active at night have mostly rods in their eyes, so they can see well in dim light. Find out what else is special about night sight.

striped skunk

If you were a skunk ...

- you would have mostly rods in your eyes, so you could see well at night.
- you would have very few cones in your eyes, so you wouldn't see color very well. You would see everything in black and white and shades of gray.

- you would have a mirrorlike layer at the back of your eyes. Light bounces off the mirror and comes back through the eye, making it glow. The extra, reflected light helps skunks to see well in the dark.

1. Have a friend hold up a colored object in a dark room or outside at night. Can you tell what color it is?

You should find that you can't see color in dim light. The cones in your eyes need light in order to work. Most nocturnal animals see the world without color.

2. Go outside on a clear night and look at the stars. Find a dim star and look directly at it. Now look just to the side of it. What do you notice?

You should find that the star looks brighter when you do not look straight at it. You have more rods at the edges of your eyes than in the middle. When you look to the side of the star, its light passes through your rods, helping you to see the star more clearly. Since nocturnal animals have more rods in their eyes than people do, they can see things more clearly at night than we can.

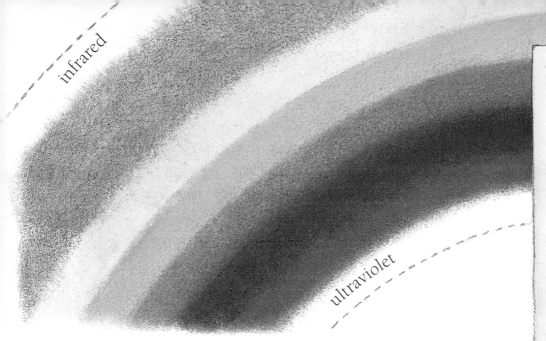

infrared

ultraviolet

Some creatures have big eyes, but not for seeing. These are special fake eyes that are used to scare away or confuse enemies or to attract mates. Look at the animals with fake eyes, or eyespots, below.

Color your world

You can see all the colors of the rainbow. Many animals can see the same colors as we can, and some can see colors that we can't. For example, rattlesnakes can see infrared, just beyond the red end of the rainbow, and insects can see ultraviolet light, past the violet end. Seeing infrared helps snakes hunt warm-bodied animals even in complete darkness. The ultraviolet markings on some flowers help a bee find the flower's nectar.

spicebush swallowtail caterpillar

polyphemus moth

A flower that looks yellow to you may look quite different to a Honey Bee.

peacock

tropical frog

15

All ears

Are your ears big or small, flat to your head or sticking out? Ears come in all shapes and sizes, from the tiny, feather-covered holes of birds to the huge flappers of elephants. No matter what they look like, ears help animals in many ways. With them animals can hear danger approaching, listen for food and water, communicate with other animals and help locate a mate. Many animals have very sensitive ears and can hear sounds that we can't. They can also move their ears around to hear better. Try wiggling your ears and then read on to find out more about some special ears.

kit fox

If you were a kit fox ...

- you would have very large, pointed ears. They would help you hear many sounds and make it easier to find and catch your food in the dark.

- you would be able to move your ears around. This would help you figure out where sounds were coming from and to hear them more clearly.

- your long ears would help you keep cool in your hot, dry, desert home, since body heat escapes through your ears faster than anywhere else.

Hear what you're missing

Have you ever watched a dog or cat perk up its ears and move them around when listening to a sound? Their large, movable ears trap more sound waves from the air and help them hear better than you can. Try on a bigger ear and hear what you're missing.

You'll need:

a piece of paper
22 cm x 27 cm
(8½ x 11 in.)

tape

music or other sounds

1. Roll the piece of paper into a cone shape and tape it. The narrow end should be big enough to fit over your outer ear.

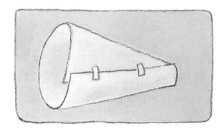

2. Hold the narrow end of the cone up to one ear. Plug the other ear with your finger.

3. Listen to some music or other sounds with the cone and without it. Point the cone away from each sound and then toward it. What do you notice?

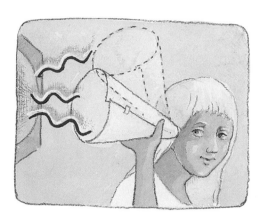

You should find that sounds seem louder with the cone. A larger ear can catch more sound waves from the air and funnel them to your eardrum, where you hear. When the cone is pointed away from the sound, the sound should seem quieter. As you turn the cone toward the sound it becomes louder. This is like a cat or dog turning its ears toward a sound to hear it better.

Ears do more than hear

Animals that live in very cold places have small ears. Small ears lose less body heat, so the animals stay warmer. An elephant's huge ears help it keep cool, and they can also scare off enemies. When an elephant flaps its big ears, other animals back off.

Sounds right (or left)

Two ears are better than one. When you hear a sound you usually hear it first in one ear and then in the other, depending on which ear is closest to the sound. This helps you tell where the sound is coming from. Animals use sound to find food and mates and to avoid danger, so locating sounds can be the key to survival. Try this simple activity to see how your ears work together.

1. Close your eyes and have a friend stand somewhere in the room and clap her hands.

2. When you hear the sound, point toward it. Have your friend move around the room and try it again a few times.

3. Now plug one of your ears with your finger and repeat the activity. Is there any difference?

You should find that it is easier to tell where the sound is coming from when both ears are working together.

Ears all over

If you think ears are always on a creature's head, then you're in for a surprise. A grasshopper's ears are on its abdomen, while crickets and katydids have ears on their legs.

Let's hear it for ears

Your ears can hear a lot of sounds, but some are too high or too low for people to hear. A cat can hear the high-pitched squeaks of an unseen mouse, and a dog will answer to a whistle that we can't hear. And don't try eavesdropping on elephants. They communicate with rumbling noises so low that people can't hear them. For some animals, hearing is more important for survival than seeing.

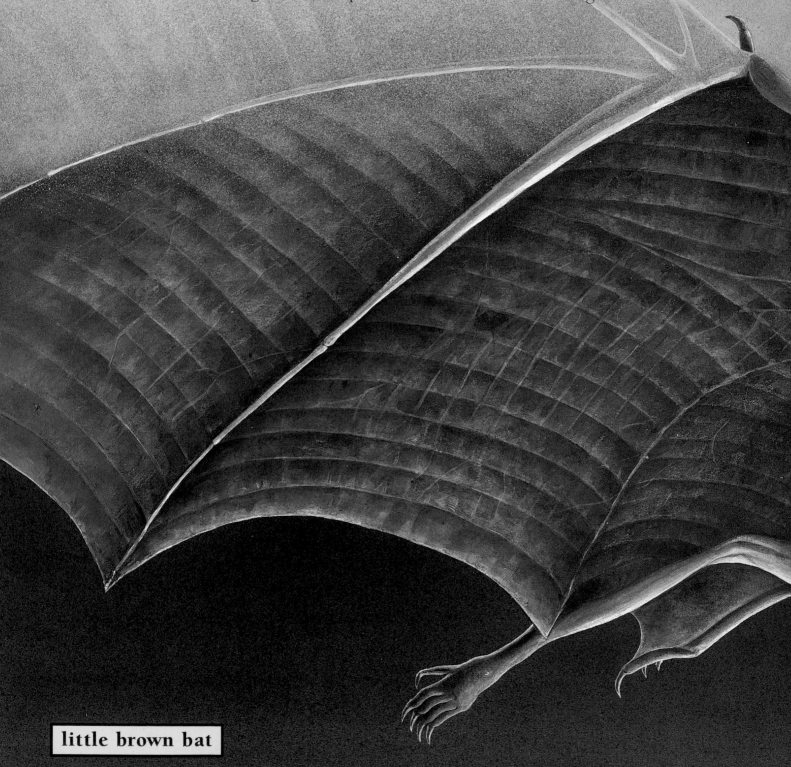

little brown bat

If you were a bat ...

• you would make very high-pitched sounds, too high for people to hear. The sounds would bounce off objects nearby and come back to your ears as echoes. The echoes would help you hunt in the dark and avoid obstacles. This is called echolocation.

• you would have large ears to hear the echoes and figure out the size, speed and location of the objects. You would be able to hear, find and catch an insect in less than half a second.

Go batty

Bats hunt by bouncing high-pitched sounds off nearby objects and listening to the echoes that come back. You can use a small rubber ball or a tennis ball to help you discover how a bat hears.

1. Stand about 2 m (6 ½ ft.) away from a wall and throw a ball at it. The ball represents the sound sent out by the bat. Notice how long it takes for the ball to come back to you. Take a large step closer to the wall and throw the ball at the same speed again. Keep moving closer to the wall and noting how long it takes the ball to return to you.

2. Have a friend hold a large board up in front of him, about 2 m (6 ½ ft.) away from you. Throw the ball at the board and notice how long it takes to come back to you. Now have your friend walk slowly toward you taking baby steps while you continue to throw the ball against the board. What do you notice?

You should find that the closer you are to the wall, the sooner the ball comes back to you. A bat can tell how close it is to an object by how quickly the echoes return to its ears. As your friend moves closer to you, the ball will come back sooner. This is how a bat can tell if an object is moving, and how quickly. Some moths can hear the bat's high-pitched sounds and drop to the ground to avoid being eaten.

Underwater echoes

Whales, dolphins and porpoises use echolocation to find food and avoid danger underwater. They make sounds that travel through the water and bounce off obstacles, fish and other creatures. By listening to the echoes, these mammals can travel safely through the water and find and catch their prey.

Feeling with sound

Some animals can sense sound even though they don't have ears. They can't hear sounds the way you do; they feel them instead. A mole doesn't have any ears, but it feels vibrations in its underground burrows. Vibrations may mean that food or danger is near. You can feel sound with this simple trick.

You'll need:
a wooden board

a hammer

Lay the board on the ground. Hold on to one end while a friend hammers on the other end. What do you feel?

You should find that you can feel the wood vibrating with your hands and hear the sound of hammering with your ears. Even if you couldn't hear, you would still feel the vibrations through the wood. If you were a mole, or another earless creature such as a snake or earthworm, you would feel the vibrations made by an approaching animal, even though you couldn't hear the sounds of its footsteps. You could tell which vibrations mean food and which ones mean danger.

The smell of survival

Even if an animal is hidden and quiet, its enemies may still find it. That's because its smell can be carried through the air. Many animals just have to sniff the wind to tell what is around. With one whiff an animal can tell if another is an enemy, a relative, a mate or a meal. A good sense of smell is very important for survival.

white-tailed deer

If you were a deer ...

- you would not give off any scent for about a week after you were born. This would keep enemies from smelling and finding you hidden in the woods or tall grass. After a week your mother would lick you all over to remove your scent before leaving you alone.

- you would have glands in your hoofs that leave a scent trail when you walk. You could always find your mother or other deer by following their scent trails.

- you would sniff the wind to find out what other animals are nearby, especially before you went out into an open field.

Take a whiff of the wind

Smells are carried by the wind. An animal sniffs the breeze to smell the scents of creatures upwind from it. The wind that blows away from an animal carries its scent to others downwind. Send out your own scents and discover the importance of being upwind or downwind.

You'll need:

dried grass or leaves
a bottle of vinegar
with a lid

1. Go outside with two friends on a breezy day and throw some dried grass or leaves up in the air. Watch to see which way they blow so you can tell the direction of the wind. Stand so that the wind is blowing on your back. You are the predator, while your friends are the prey. Have one friend stand about 2 m (6 1/2 ft.) behind you and the other 2 m (6 1/2 ft.) in front of you.

2. Open the bottle of vinegar and hold it out to your side so the fumes (your scent) escape easily. Have each friend yell when they first smell the vinegar.

You should find that the friend in front of you, or downwind from you, was the first to smell the

vinegar. As soon as that prey could smell you, it would leave. Your friend who is upwind could not smell the vinegar. You would be able to sneak up on that prey. When an animal is hunting, it is careful to stay downwind of its prey to avoid detection.

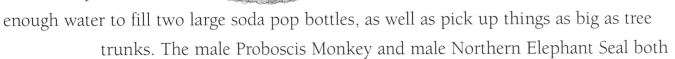

Super Sniffers

Imagine having a nose over 2 m (6½ ft.) long, like an elephant's! Not only is it a super sniffer, it's useful for many other things too. An elephant's trunk can suck up and hold enough water to fill two large soda pop bottles, as well as pick up things as big as tree trunks. The male Proboscis Monkey and male Northern Elephant Seal both have enormous noses. Their huge noses make their voices louder and deeper which may attract mates and scare off enemies more easily.

You can see how the size of your nose affects how you sound. Speak normally and then pinch your nose to make it smaller while you continue speaking. What do you hear? You should find that your voice has a slightly higher pitch when your nose is pinched.

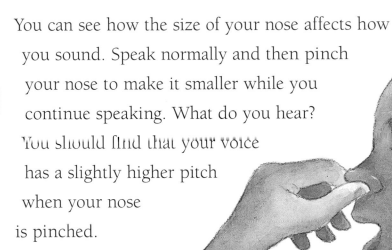

Not just noses

Nosing around comes naturally to you, but how do animals without noses smell? Insects smell with their antennae, and catfish use their whiskers and barbels for picking up scents on a lake bottom or riverbed. An octopus smells and tastes with its tentacles. When a snake sticks out its tongue, it's collecting scent particles from the air.

Say it with a smell

You can tell what mood your friend is in by what she says
or how she looks, but what about by the way she smells?
Animals use sounds and sights to communicate, but smells
are also very important for sending messages. If you've
ever smelled a skunk's spray, you probably got the message
"stay away" loud and clear. Read on to find out more
about speaking with smells.

Animals that live together in groups use smell to identify
members of their own group. A mother antelope not
only recognizes the scent of her herd, she can also find
the special smell of her young within the herd.

When a female moth is ready to mate she releases a special scent to attract a male. Some male moths can smell a female more than five average city blocks away.

People put up No Trespassing signs when they want other people to stay away. If you were a fox you would leave smells to warn others not to come near. These animals urinate on trees or rocks around their territory to let other foxes know that the land is occupied.

When an ant finds food, it lets other ants know by passing along scent messages with its antennae. The ant also leaves a scent trail between the colony and the food so other ants can find their way.

How sweet it is

Are there foods that you really like and others you'd rather not eat? Wild animals also have favorite foods. Many caterpillars eat only one kind of plant, and birds won't eat Monarch butterflies because of their bad taste. Cats can't taste sweet things at all. Your taste buds are on your tongue, but you may be surprised to find out what body parts other animals use for tasting.

European swallowtail butterfly

If you were a butterfly ...

- you would have taste buds on your feet. You'd walk around on a flower before deciding if it was good enough to eat.

- your tongue would be coiled up like a party blower under your head. To feed, your tongue would straighten out like a straw and suck up the flower's sweet nectar.

- you would be two hundred times more sensitive to sweet things than a human is.

A tasty test

Compare how you and a butterfly taste sweet things with this simple experiment.

You'll need:

water

an empty 2-L (8-c.) bottle

a large, clean bucket or basin

sugar

a large spoon

a bowl

1. Pour 6 bottles of water into the bucket. Stir in 15 mL (1 tbsp.) of sugar.

2. Taste the sugar solution. Can you taste the sweetness in the water?

3. Now pour 60 mL (¼ c.) of water into a bowl and add 15 mL (1 tbsp.) of sugar. Stir well and then taste the sugar solution. How does it compare to the solution in the bucket? This solution is about two hundred times sweeter than the bucket solution.

You should find that the sugar solution in the bucket did not taste sweet because there was so little sugar compared to the amount of water. The solution in the bowl should have tasted very sweet. It is hard for you to taste the sweetness in the bucket solution, but a butterfly would find it very sweet. In fact, it would taste as sweet to the butterfly as the solution in the bowl tasted to you.

Tasting without tongues

Butterflies, moths and flies taste with their feet, and many other insects taste with their antennae. Mussels and scallops test their food with their tentacles. If you were a catfish you could tell if something was good to eat by swimming close to it, because your body would be covered with taste buds.

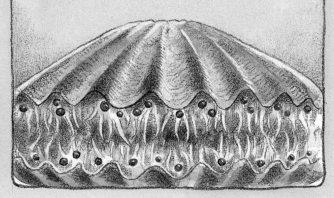

Talented tongues

Pour some milk into a saucer and try lapping it up the way a cat does. It's not as easy as it sounds. A cat's tongue is very rough so the milk "holds on" to the tongue as the cat drinks. Cats also use their tongues to clean and brush their fur. Check out the other talented tongues on this page.

A giraffe's tongue is protected from the sun with a natural sunscreen while it picks leaves from the treetops.

Woodpeckers have extra long, sticky tongues that are perfect for catching insects for food.

Snails have toothy tongues for shredding plants before eating them.

Lizards use their tongues to clean their eyes.

A toad's tongue is attached at the front of its mouth so it can flip out a long way to catch a tasty fly.

Keep in touch

When you sit down to supper you can see what you're eating, but what if you had to feel what was on your plate to tell if it was edible or not? Many animals use their sense of touch to find and identify food before they eat it. Touch is also important for getting around in the dark, for finding shelter and mates and for avoiding danger.

walrus

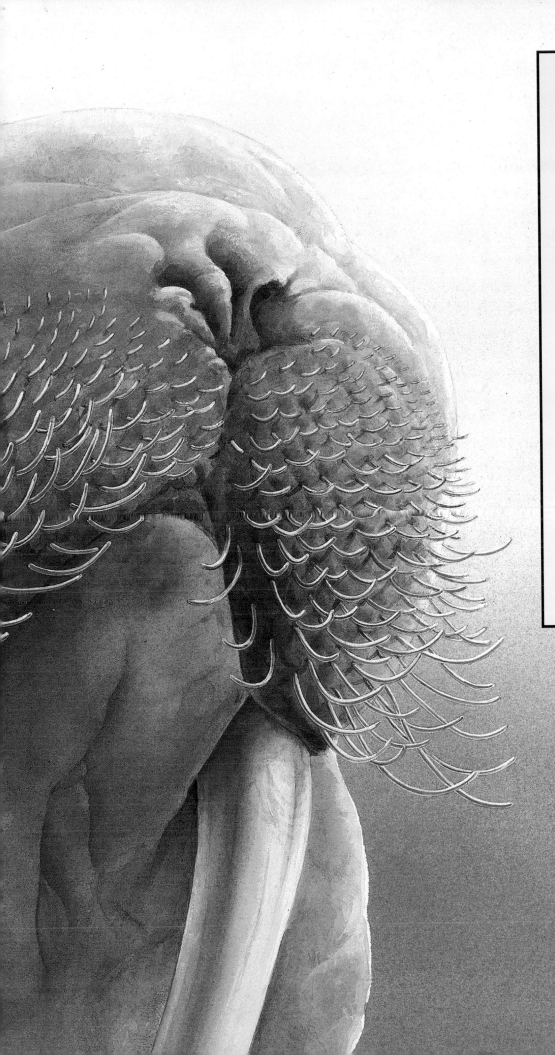

If you were a walrus ...

- you'd have rows of stiff whiskers around your mouth for feeling.

- you'd poke your whiskers into the muddy ocean bottom to feel for food. When you found something the right shape and texture — such as a clam or crab — you'd dig it out with your tusks and eat it.

Feel for your food

Invite a friend over for lunch and have him feel for his food, like a walrus.

3. Blindfold your friend and have him poke his fingers into the bowl and identify the objects he feels. He should pull out only the edible items, as a walrus does.

You should find that common objects are not too difficult to identify, but some food items may be harder because you are not used to feeling them without seeing them at the same time. Your fingers are acting like the whiskers of the walrus, feeling for food you can't see.

1. Fill a large bowl or bucket with sand or soil.

4. Have your friend bury different objects in the container for you to identify.

2. Bury the objects in the container.

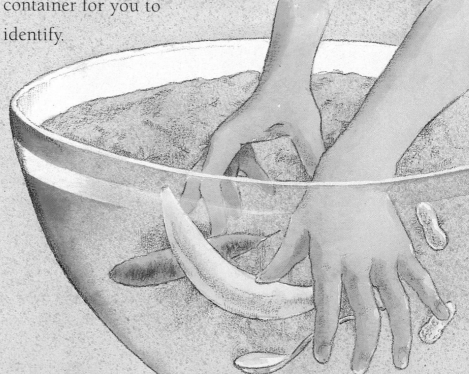

Feeling safe

Your fingertips are the most sensitive part of your body. Other animals use different body parts for feeling. A cat's whiskers are terrific feelers, insects have sensitive body hairs and birds use their feathers as feelers. No matter what they use to feel with, animals rely on their sense of touch to help them avoid danger. Slugs and snails avoid heat and sharp, dry surfaces that can dry out their bodies or cut their soft foot. The Starnose Mole has tentacle-like feelers around its snout that help the animal find its way through dark, 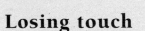 underground tunnels and keep it from going out into the open where it might be seen by an enemy.

Some animals and plants survive by being "untouchable." The prickles of a porcupine keep most predators far away. The stings of bees and wasps make insect eaters stay clear. Even prickly or thorny plants are too painful for plant eaters to munch on.

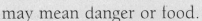

Losing touch

When you put on your clothes in the morning you feel them against your skin, but after a few minutes you no longer notice them. That's because your sense of touch grows tired when it is constantly stimulated by the same thing. Being able to ignore the feel of consistent touches helps an animal focus on new feelings that may mean danger or food.

Surprising senses

In addition to the five basic senses of sight, hearing, smell, taste and touch, some animals have supersenses that can detect things people can't. Imagine having a built-in compass so that you'd never get lost, or being able to feel the electricity given off by an approaching friend. Read on to find out more about these surprising senses.

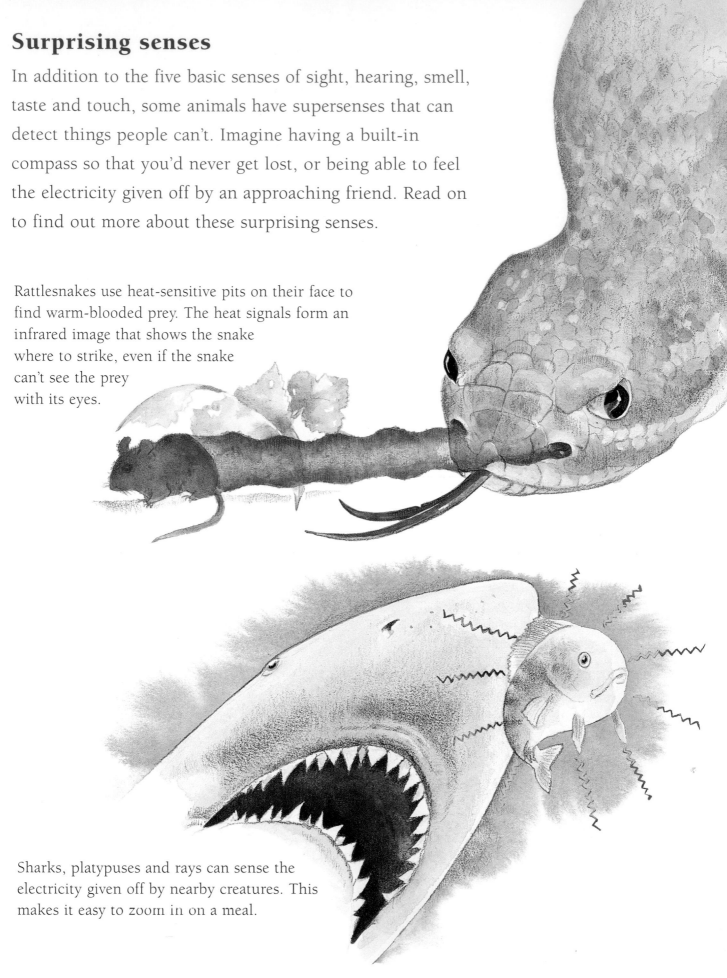

Rattlesnakes use heat-sensitive pits on their face to find warm-blooded prey. The heat signals form an infrared image that shows the snake where to strike, even if the snake can't see the prey with its eyes.

Sharks, platypuses and rays can sense the electricity given off by nearby creatures. This makes it easy to zoom in on a meal.

Migrating birds have a built-in compass that can detect the magnetic field of Earth. This helps them know what direction to fly in.

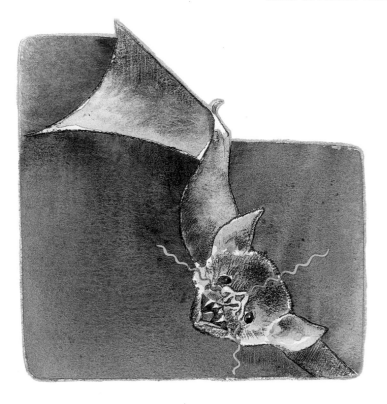

Bloodsucking animals, such as mosquitoes and vampire bats, have built-in heat sensors to help locate warm-bodied animals to feed on.

Superhuman senses

You may not be able to see heat images the way a rattlesnake does, but with the help of infrared photography it is possible to take heat pictures of hidden, warm-blooded creatures. People have invented some amazing tools, such as microscopes, telescopes, X-ray machines, ultrasound, lasers and metal detectors, to help us extend our senses beyond our natural limits.

Index

Answers

Page 10
The predators are the lynx, wolf and bear.